My Father in Water

Also by Carol Guess

Poetry
Doll Studies: Forensics Black Lawrence Press, forthcoming
Love Is A Map I Must Not Set On Fire VRZHU Press, 2009
Tinderbox Lawn Rose Metal Press, 2008
Femme's Dictionary Calyx Books, 2004

Fiction
Darling Endangered Brooklyn Arts Press, forthcoming
Willful Machine PS Publishing, forthcoming
Homeschooling PS Publishing, 2010
Switch Calyx Books, 1998
Seeing Dell Cleis Press, 1996

Other
Gaslight (memoir) Odd Girls Press, 2001

Carol Guess

My Father in Water

Shearsman Books

First published in the United Kingdom in 2011 by
Shearsman Books
58 Velwell Road
Exeter EX4 4LD

www.shearsman.com

ISBN 978-1-84861-185-6

Contents

One

Two

Three

To the memory of my father, Harry A. Guess

ONE

Aperture

In a photograph taken when I was two, I'm sitting in the drawer of a filing cabinet playing with my toes. A dog-eared sticker on the front of the drawer reads *Radioactive* and I am, I glow. I glow blonde, white-blonde, sun-slashed, contented. I am a West Coast baby sitting in a filing cabinet marked *Radioactive*, waiting on a difficult father who scrawls numbers in chalk. He, in turn, is waiting on a difficult admiral to tell him whether some submarine will sink or swim.

Days, my father feeds cards into a computer the size of our home, cards he carries home for me to color. Nights, I do not have a sister and I do not dream of the sister I'll have. Oh, the years without her, the time when I am the center of two beautiful, terrible attention spans! My father vanishes, returns, vanishes again. He begins to make numbers mean important things.

I am two. I am almost a Christmas baby, almost a tax break. My sister is not yet born, not yet conceived. When she is born, she will take over, occupying space with miniature authority, a lazy ease passers-by will call *adorable*. I will be bald, still. Mistaken for a boy. I will bypass *adorable* and go straight to *clever*.

Later, when my mother feeds me fish, I will spit it out and stuff it in my sister's mouth.

But just then I am glowing, radioactive. My father is watching a sub fill with water. My mother is not ready for her father to die.

Most beautiful is my mother in photos with cats, her thick black eyeliner incautiously feline. I am the one with the Cheshire smile—at two, even.

My father frowns.

My sister is not yet born.

When they play Muzak at the naval base, the admiral sends out a call. A phone rings. Doors slam. A messenger appears out of nowhere, sprinting. Rips out the speaker above each door on the hall.

(Years later, during a fight over gays in the military: *Those submarines*, my father says, *are very small*.)

But I'm not yet gay. I love only my toes, and my difficult father, and my porcelain mother. At night my father vanishes, or goes stone, or plays Linda Ronstadt, The Beatles, and Elton John. *Rock me on the ramble, Rocket Man. Lucy in the wings with the walrus hammer.*

I love my parents and they love me. I wear pink flowery nightgowns, although my mother later erases this memory, finding it easier to remember her dyke daughter in PJs. I name our first cat after my favorite food: spaghetti with meatballs. And our second cat after my second favorite: spaghetti with meatballs. They become Meatballs One and Meatballs Two, then One and Two, then *was* and *were*.

By then I have a sister. And she is more beautiful than I, ahead of me already, and she thinks this of me, and so we learn to hate women.

❖

But that's not the story I meant to tell. The story I meant to tell has no beginning and no end and runs underneath the story of my sister like a river. My father hovers in the aperture of a glistening window, suicide botched by his mother's ghost. Numbers from his slide rule pause on the sill, fallen by chance into a brilliant formula.

My mother walks to school in a flour sack printed with pansies, her German accent smeared with eggs. Her last name means *graveyard circled with trees*. Verbs dawdle between the gaps in her teeth.

My parents, speaking German in a German café, capitalizing every noun carefully, making new words from old, homesick at last. My parents in Heidelberg, only not yet my parents. Harold Adelbert, meet Geraldine Ann. She's shy, her hands covering uneven teeth. He's an engineer geek: highwaters, pocket protector. Both speak fluently but neither fools the other. American-born, they'll return to different worlds. After Heidelberg their courtship is epistolary, a literary romance I'll never read. Geraldine's father Stanley burns their love letters. *Ravish*. Oh mother! *Your slender hands.*

And she becomes a navy wife.

And he thinks he's finally escaped the South.

And she hopes someday to become middle class.

And he becomes acquainted with great tenderness.

During Vietnam he works at Naval Reactors among a tight-knit, top-secret gaggle of math majors. He helps design nuclear submarines, the first of many dramatic careers. So much to discover, so many numbers to love! His brief forays away from theory end in dismay as he encounters humans.

But numbers and power, the great nuclear mystery. I am born to a genius no one can take anywhere, who scrawls formulas on tablecloths in fancy restaurants and doesn't look either way when crossing the street. Occasionally he forgets his address and thumbs through the phone book to call home and ask.

My mother manages him; this becomes her career. Over the years she learns piles of secrets. Discoveries yield to her as she tends to their maker. She arranges father, business, and us.

Carol Ann, meet Alison Pauline.

In pictures I hate her. They've obviously made me hold her; I'm posed like a doll. My sister's face lolls up at me, happy. She's always drooling; my eyes look crazed.

And I think she's more beautiful.

And she thinks I'm ahead.

And I long for the *friend* my mother promised.

And she's shamed by my difference: *freak, slut, queer.*

No one should have a sibling. What an impossible relation, an arranged marriage, maybe worse. This person, your blood, no one you've chosen.

And we want to love each other.

And we try until it turns to rage.

Little Trimesters, little sisters. Two girls, unlucky, stars burning too brightly. Strange family, with a hole at its center. I am trying to make sense of my distant father. *Very good, Carol.*

Carol, be still. At school I'm already becoming the sea.

Shy girl, to whom numbers mean nothing. Holding the clock to my forehead, my tongue. Unable to match minutes to hours. Dreaming already, little poems about ghosts.

My sister flits past me, grown-up already. Boys like a beacon in her version of night. I slide through the holes in my parents' stories, past the blue before speech to which I try to return.

Red

I am fifteen and I have no name, but I am learning how to get into a car without showing my underwear to the men surrounding me.

A woman is teaching me.

She has long nails, a short skirt, willowy heels.

"Girls," she says. There are ten of us in beauty school, thirteen to thirty-nine. "Girls, pretend you are surrounded by handsome men. One of them opens the car door for you. How do you enter?"

I begin by imagining the men in great detail. I give them faces and names because one of them might be my husband. When it's my turn, I totter in my spiky heels to the center of the circle. I sit in the passenger seat, my back to the driver, and swing my legs gracefully, torso twisting in sync.

"Now get out," she says.

And later: *remember to keep your knees shut tight, like a secret you can't tell.* Her nails are red. One of the men I imagine is real. He has a name and a face and a zippy red car. He is ten years older than me, and a bad driver.

After everyone has had her turn in and out of the car, we leave the parking garage and return to the classroom. One by one we strip to our underwear, step on the scale, and sink.

Think about numbers for the first time that week.

When I step on the scale, the women surround me. I feel their stares like heat on my shoulders and thighs. One writes the number in a folder; another tugs on her straps—powder blue. There is so much lace in the room. It makes me happy. At fifteen I like lace and complicated colors—mauve, violet, silver. I like frills and words such as "full-face" and "uplift." They assuage my fears that I do not fit in, fears I cannot name because I cannot point to anything different about me. I look like all the other fifteen-year-olds at my high school: thin, diffident, pastel. We are all anorexic and painfully, almost parodically, feminine. We look like drag queens, except for Jessica, a star on the swim team.

She looks like a linebacker.

I avoid her.

My locker is covered with pictures of ballerinas. At fifteen, for reasons I can't explain, I flip through dance magazines, culling pictures of muscular male stars, which I paste carefully over the bodies of Suzanne Farrell, Kyra Nichols, and Heather Watts. When I get to my favorite photo, of Heather Watts twisted into a pretzel, I can't bring myself to cover her with Peter Martins. Instead I leave her, a tiny woman with legs muscled into perfect figure eights, suspended like a question. I also pin up pictures of girls I dance with, their legs twisted into cautious letters. I would like a picture of the man with the red car, but he laughs when I say I want one for my locker.

When he calls, my mother summons me from the bedroom lair where I am sprawled on my bed eating rice cakes and drinking diet soda. She murmurs his name in a studied whisper, but her eyes betray her pleasure. Because I don't have make-up on, I feel self-conscious. I twirl my hair around my finger and shift from foot to foot.

He is a bad driver because I distract him.

At least, this is what he tells me. But when I say *sorry*, he puts his hand on my thigh and twists the steering wheel in an abrupt, deliberate jerk. He was my brother's babysitter last summer, while my parents were in Europe and I was at dance camp. My brother liked him, his roguishness, the thick shock of pale hair falling over his left eye. They played good games, my brother says—catch and half-court and Pac Man—and ate McDonalds six nights out of nine. He was a good babysitter, my parents agree, and when he calls to ask if I want to go for a walk in Larrett Park one Saturday, I imagine we will play good games, too.

Thirty minutes before he arrives at the house, I am lounging in my bedroom, biting my nails and reading teen magazine articles on bulimia. I am thinking about throwing up, how it would feel, what my mouth would taste like after. In one story a girl eats half a cake and two pints of ice cream before she lets the food slide from her gut to her throat to her lips, then rejects it. I love the articles, love the descriptions before the girl vomits—the decadence of the orgy, the long lists of forbidden foods.

I am daydreaming about ice cream when my mother knocks. She looks startled to find that I am in my nightgown. Her whole face contracts into a clock. "He'll be here in half an hour," she says, folding her hands over and over. They look like water as she waves me into the bathroom, as she sits me on the toilet lid and begins to do my face.

When the man with the red car arrives, I am ready. I am wearing a short black skirt safety-pinned around my thinning middle, a long velour black sweater, and a gargantuan pink bow at the back of my head. My bracelets and earrings make a great deal of noise as we walk around the park. Once I burp. I am mortified. He pretends not to hear and when no one is looking, plucks a rare flower and tucks it behind my ear.

In beauty school I am learning about illusion—how to create the simulacrum of depth. When I make up my lips I use a pale, creamy base to destroy their actual shape, so that the face in the classroom mirror has no mouth. Then I outline a new set of lips with brick-red pencil and fill in the outline with movie-star red. For the finale, I smudge a dab of light pink in line with my nose, at the center of the bow-shape everyone in class is envious of.

Once I emerge with a spectacular Betty Boop smirk that Tara, our Tri-Delta, singles out with the right index finger of her French manicure. "You look twenty-one," she says, her voice a mixture of envy and something else. I don't like the envy, but I like her gesture, which happens in slow motion. I even remember touch, soft soft at my skin, but perhaps I made that up, or make it up now—me, Carol, the storyteller.

The day of our walk in the park, our first time alone together, the man with the red car drops me off in time for dinner. I thank him and ask if he'd like to come inside and visit my brother.

He is, after all, the babysitter.

He cocks his head. His right eye is autumn-amber. "I didn't come for your brother," he says. And he reaches for my lips with his whole hand.

After our lessons, after we have created our faces for the week, we put cheesecloth bags over our heads before we tug our smocks off. The bags emerge stained with cheeks, eyes, lips as the pink of our smocks is replaced by cool tans and crisp navys. We learn to fix snags in our hose with nail polish, spreading the sticky stuff over the runs carefully, without concern for the flesh beneath. We learn to fix anything that runs, sags, or bleeds with acrylic and cotton, bobby pins and saccharine.

Every week we weigh ourselves. Although I hate the scale's bold proclamations, hate the tears of the women who have come for this reason, I love the flowers we become when we strip down to our bras and panties. The older women wear sophisticated colors—greens, grays, violets that shimmer when they brush past me, biting their lips. We leave our jewelry on, but not our heels; they lie jumbled in a pile like obscure weaponry. Once, as I am tugging my skirt back over my hips, Tara leans towards me, still shirtless, and congratulates me on losing another pound. In the grace of her gesture I see only a shadow, the faint darkness of a line where her cream-colored push-up bra cups meet in a satin bow. My difference is there, in that moment; though I write it off as envy, as wanting to be like Tara, some part of my mind knows it is something else.

In the lunchroom at school, Jessica passes my table carrying a tray filled with food. My friends and I tug the foil tops off plain yogurt, exchange carrot sticks, sip diet soda through bendable straws. When Jessica returns for seconds before Nancy has even finished her symmetrical apple slices, Claire nudges me and I take care of it.

"*Hungry*," I hiss. The other girls pick it up. *Hungry*, then *Greedy*, then, although Jessica is muscular, a swimmer, *Fatty*.

Fatty becomes *Lezzie*.

And I am safe.

In beauty school I am learning about perspective. One day my teacher, Glory Sue, hands me a bra with breasts already in it. They are flesh-colored, though not the color of my flesh, mottled pink and freckled, nor the color of Jasmine's, dark brown with red undertones, but the fragile jaundice-yellow of a sickly baby, whiny and urine-scented, longing for milk. The cloth around the breasts is red—red satin—and Glory Sue winks as she hands it over. When I fold it double, the cups make a hand puppet, red mouth without a voice. Years later, I find it wadded in the back of my dresser and tie it to a doorknob, knowing my cat will show no mercy, knowing that animals use things in useful ways.

He parks the red car where no one will see its color. He wanted hunter or pewter, something masculine, something stark. Instead there is this red, and me, spread open. I watch the stars through the window when I'm on my back. On my belly, there's nothing to see, so I close my eyes. Once, in the middle of a contortion, he bursts out laughing. When I sit up, frightened, he is holding the red bra.

When he drops me off, the house is dark. In the morning I eat breakfast with my brother, who calls me a slut until our mother shushes him.

At Christmas the man with the red car's parents give me a necklace—a tiny amber bead encased in gold. They hand me the package, then go into the living room and drink cocktails with my parents. When I show my mother the necklace, she holds it in her palm for a long while. There is something else in her eyes; I can't name it. When she gives it back, the amber feels warm.

When the man with the red car comes to our door, my mother checks my make-up and my father hands me money. Every week, excluding holidays, I earn ten dollars because I pocket the cash. It's meant to cover the usual fancies. But the man with the red car pays for everything, so I think of my time with him as free.

He comes. My parents welcome him. Often he sits inside for several minutes, joshing about stock options, baseball, films. He is serious and pseudo-intellectual, which suits his startling eyes and golden hair. He lives with his parents because he is struggling to open his own law business—at twenty-five, no less! *Wunderkind*, my parents joke when they think I can't hear them. They both kiss my forehead before I leave the house. They don't wait up, but they show their concern for our safety—his as well as mine—in the bend that signals *kiss*. Then my father opens the door and everyone watches as I leave the house first. Once, when I turn back, the man with the red car is standing between my parents, the longed-for son of their senior years.

He opens the car door for me. I totter in my spiky heels to the car's gaping red mouth. I sit in the passenger seat, my back to the driver, and swing my legs gracefully, torso twisting in sync.

"Now get out," he says later. We are parked in a deserted lot. The railway station shimmers, ghostly; I will remember its faint outlines better than his hands. I will remember the ghostly silhouettes of buildings, benches, tracks, and the whistle of the trains that pass by but don't stop. Years later, when I see steamed-up cars, I will wonder if the girl waited for her date to open her door and help her out, then into the backseat; if the seat belts left bruises; if the radio was on.

Sometimes he says my name.

At first I don't understand that the moment of naming precedes expulsion. I think that my name, shifting between his lips, is a gift, a moment of identification. But the name is a release, a rush of air that parallels the rush his body makes, all strength and density. No part of me admires it; there is nothing beautiful in it, though years later I will fall in love with a man and try to understand what he calls *pleasure*. But for now there is only the dark triangle his body makes, hovering, and his words, sounds really, letters chosen not for meaning but for motion.

Sometimes he says my name, but that name never reaches the world beyond his car. In school I take a nickname, while he calls me by my birth name. In school the kids call me *Kate* and the letters do not remind me of him.

I am safe. And thin. In beauty school we fix dinner at the end of every lesson—vegetables wilting like sylphs dying onstage. We eat carefully, admiring each other's manners, sticking to the assigned topics: movies, weather, domesticated animals, art.

And Him.

"The key to a successful date is to make him feel like a Great Man."

We learn to listen to men, to nod, to agree. We learn *yes yes yes* and *thank you please*.

Years later I take a self-defense class. The first thing the instructor asks us to do is scream. Around me women open their mouths and form the nameless syllables that signify fear. I open my mouth, too, widening the lips my grandmother bequeathed me, the bow-shaped lips that are the only thing linking me to her ghost, to the woman I believe would have understood me. I open my mouth and inhale, silent.

The instructor is gentle with me. But I leave the class crying because I cannot scream.

The man with the red car makes small talk with me, shies away from anything serious. Once I mention the word abortion and he frowns, so I know exactly how he feels. I am in tune with him, with his red car; I am empathetic and sympathetic both; I make him feel a Great Man. In turn, he tells me I am beautiful, desirable, a rare flower.

But in the mirror at school, I do not look beautiful. His stubbled cheeks leave scratches, as if someone has struck a match against my skin. I am thin, thinner, thinnest. My friends and I pretend not to notice as each of us picks at her lunch.

One day I am in the bathroom, redoing my lips—two colors only, I do not have time for my mouth to vanish and return— when Jessica bustles in. I pretend I'm not watching as she rummages for change.

When her search fails, when her palms come up empty from her pockets, she turns to me and asks for what she needs in a surprisingly soft, low voice.

I am startled. No one—not one of my friends—still bleeds. No one weighs enough. It is understood that to bleed is to be fat.

I put the cap on my lipstick. She is looking at me and when I turn away from her eyes in the mirror, I look at the floor. It will be years before I understand that the something else she sees in my eyes before I turn away, the gaze that takes in her solid body, her incautious gestures, her gentle muscularity, is desire.

Yes yes yes.

Thank you.

I do.

Sometimes he asks why I'm so quiet. Once, we watch a film in which the heroine whispers sexy things to her husband. After the film is over, he picks at his hamburger.

"Can't you be more like that?"

I try.

I try to speak, to say things that will light the dark hum of the red car. But years later, in college, four boys will surround me on a dark walkway, surround me and begin, inexplicably, to tickle, then kiss me. The kisses will feel sharp, like needle pricks. And I will stand, shouting distance from a clump of passerby, shouting distance from students clustered at the steps of the library, and my throat will dry and my body will harden and I will not be able to make the sounds that might save me.

In school I stop speaking. My teachers appreciate my polite, discreet presence. My teachers are men, and we do not read books by women. The women in the books we do read are quiet—victims, mothers, maids. My teachers tell me I am a good listener. They suggest I apply to Ivy League schools like other promising students, white, wealthy students, students who have attended private schools like mine, students like me.

Somehow I doubt the existence of others like me.

But I hide my sense of my difference. When my teachers comment admiringly on my poise, my sweetness, my dresses, I smile, knowing perfectly well by now what effect that has. I am a dancer. I know how to work an audience. At night, in the red car, I perform.

My real self, the girl between two names, is somewhere else.

Years later I will find that place useful for hiding, for avoiding the reality of a lover who has changed, her face mirroring the man who has stolen from her what I am also missing. The something else in her eyes will shift and smoke, becoming fear. I will watch her as she hovers over me, a dark triangle, watch my lover become the thing I am most afraid of, simply because she is afraid of me.

I will fantasize about killing him, her father. I will fantasize about it in great detail, until one day in my fantasy his face, the face I know only from photographs, becomes the face of the man with the red car.

At home, in the vestibular space of my bedroom, between my parents' world, the red car, dancing, and school, I write poems. In the poems I am water, and the man with the red car is a duck. I slide down his back in drops.

In my journal I write that I love him, that I want to marry him.

And so I stop eating, because I cannot find a way to reconcile the worlds I inhabit, and because starvation is the only speech I can afford.

Sometimes, like the goose girl in my favorite fairy tale, I speak to a familiar, hoping my familiar will answer. One day I am talking to the man with the red car. He is eating a sundae and I am watching. I ask him one of the questions they've taught us in beauty school: *if you were an animal, what would you be?*

He does not have to think it over. "A squirrel," he says, and I can tell he's proud. He slurps the last of his sundae through a straw. He does not ask what I would be.

I think to myself, *I would be a man.*

It is 1986. When I move to New York City for college, I find it smeared in blood. There are bloody handprints everywhere, prints of names, names of politicians. I read the posters as I rush to the studio each morning—*Mayor Koch, Our Blood Is On Your Hands*, then a logo I don't understand, a pale pink triangle. *Act Up* it says, and *Silence Equals Death*. But death feels far away; silence, necessary.

In college I study English with a Great Man. I love his excitement at a strong line, a keen metaphor. I love his excitement, but when I whisper this to the girl next to me, he slams his hand on the podium angrily.

"I won't have you talking about me," he says, his voice husky with cigarettes. Later, I learn that he is sleeping with her. He praises her body to us on the many days that she is absent.

After class, girls whisper to each other: *don't let him shut the door to his office when he asks you in.* When the Great Man asks me in, I stand in the crevice the door makes, triangular, afraid of the bright light of his desk lamp and the blue light of his eyes. He hands me a copy of his latest book, then summons me closer so he can sign it. The book is complicated and clever; inside the word *lips* appears many times.

I take four classes with him so that I can learn to be a writer. We do not read a single woman author. Once someone asks why, waving his arm from the back row like an alarm that has suddenly decided to go off.

The Great Man answers without losing his place in *The Waste Land*. "There are no British or American women writers worth reading."

"Dickinson?"

"Too domestic."

"Plath?"

"Too angry."

"Woolf?"

"Derivative."

"Stein?"

He laughs. "I think Stein's problem is self-evident."

I am sitting two rows from the front, vibrating with a new understanding of how a poem is composed. The Great Man has given me Stevens; he has given me Pound. He has also taught me the difference between bad and good poetry. When he asks us to write for his class, I know that I must not write about the man with the red car. That would be an angry poem, or maybe a domestic poem, or, worse, an angry domestic poem. That would be, I now know, a bad poem.

Instead I write sonnets about clouds, six each semester. Twenty-four poems about terrible weather. Sometimes, while I am writing, my pen skids to a stop before *nimbus*, before *cumulus*. Sometimes I see no point in finishing that week's poem, however fluffy the cloud, however silver its lining, simply because I am a woman, and women, as I now know, write bad poetry.

I get an A.

One of the boys asks me what I did to make the grade.

At night, after class, I ride the subway to my apartment. One of the girls from class rides as far as my stop. Often we sit across from each other, acknowledging each other's presence only by proximity. I know she sees me; I know she knows that I see her.

It takes me a month to realize who she reminds me of.

By then I feel it, the something else I cannot name. There are jokes—gay people call it gaydar—about the thrill and terror of recognition, about its power. But there is no proper name for what I feel and, without a name, without witness, Jessica's bond with me vanishes, becomes wholly body, body and then energy, energy and then vibration, motion without signifier, unrecordable.

I do not see her.

The joke goes, "She could've saved you five years."

But I deny her. I turn from Jessica's new incarnation, this woman who sees through me, who inspires in me a charged knowledge that elaborates, magically, on something I do not yet claim. She sits across from me on the subway, dyke Christ to my Judas, vowing to haunt me. And I see Jessica after Jessica, year after year, until I finally give in and open my mouth in an ecstatic communion.

I come to hate studying. Thin, too thin, I have trouble concentrating. Words waver in front of my eyes. When I faint, the stairs to my brownstone redden and dissolve to dark.

For several days I cannot leave my apartment. Every time I begin a task, fears stall me, until unlocking the door is impossible. I pace, taking pieces of myself apart, until I am saved by a crack whore.

Her name is Corinne.

Her name is Corinne, and she lives down the hall. I know she is a whore because her clients ride the elevator with her, and because her pimp stalks her. Once, I step off the elevator to find him pounding on her door, first with a folding chair, then with his thick body.

"Corinne, goddammit, open the fucking door! Prazzie wants to see you, you shitty slut. Corinne!"

I know she's on crack because she buys in the park two blocks away, out in the open the way crack deals happen in my neighborhood, her palm glowing with light, with the tiny glass vials.

The week I cannot leave my apartment, Corinne breaks the spell, pounding on my door one sweaty midnight. Her desperation does something to my nervous obsessiveness and I open the door in a rush of glad freedom. All she wants is rubbing alcohol. In exchange, she lets me visit her apartment to see her murphy bed and seven cats.

I tell the man with the red car that there will be no more visits. His phone calls stalk me, plaintive and poignant, his grief at our break-up similar to the sound of the girls I dance with when they puke in the sink. Eventually the calls stop and the lies begin—lies to my parents, who still hope for a wedding.

I am distracted for the next several years. The man with the red car has distracted me. But I do not blame him. I look at my lips in the mirror—bow-shaped, like my grandmother's. She was a singer, but instead of a voice, she bequeathed me her lips.

Her name was Buena Vista—*good view.*

Her marriage to my grandfather saved the family farm.

I like my lips. I do not blame him, the man with the red car, for wanting to touch them. I look in the mirror every morning before I make up my face with all that red. Sometimes, thinking of Tara, I touch myself.

The smile I see isn't mine.

It will be years before I bleed again, before the color red means something else. It will be years before I drive myself, long hours on a deserted highway, to see a woman with red hair. It will be years before someone watches me eat, watches my lips with a stare that is neither calculated nor appraising, but wicked. It will be years before wickedness appeals to me, before I stop wearing pink, before a red car means little or nothing, before the face in the mirror opens its plain mouth to speak.

"Do you have anything darker?" my girlfriend asks the skeptical blonde behind the counter. We are shopping for lipstick because I want to kiss her and leave prints.

"I'll go check," the salesgirl says, and heads for the back of the store.

She does not return.

So we steal things—silver eyeliner, blue nail polish, men's cologne. For a week, on a dare, my lover and I wear blue nail polish until it scabs off and we find ourselves picking at it with our teeth. But for that week, her hands on my flesh look like bruises, as if someone has hit my thighs, arms, belly. Her hands on my flesh look ugly, and I beg her to remove the color, to make her nails clear again.

For our beauty school graduation dinner, we're instructed to bring something fattening—something *sinful*, Glory Sue says. I bake a pumpkin pie. When it is cool, I cover it in plastic, tucking in its edges.

Years later, I will enter my lover's kitchen, lured by a sweet, cinnamon scent, buttery and warm. "Pie," she says. "Sweet potato." We stand in the kitchen, sipping coffee, waiting for it to cool. When it is done, she cuts two large slices and motions me to join her. She walks through the kitchen, living room, hallway. I follow her, and I follow the pie. She pushes open the door to our bedroom with her shoulder, flicks the light with her wrist. Then she sets both plates on the bedstand and sits on the quilt.

The slices are wrapped; for a moment I think she wants me to touch and taste through plastic. Instead she smiles, removing the barrier.

The beauty school classroom mirrors are veiled in gauzy streamers; at the center of the room is a table draped in silver cloth. We place our pies, cakes, cookies, and pastries in a seductive chorus line and then stand, soldiers at a peep show.

We wait for the word.

Eat.

We expect to hear it any minute. But we are well-trained; we do not flinch. We watch each other through the streamer-draped mirror and we do not know that we are watching hunger.

Glory Sue hands each of us a rolled-up certificate, stamped with a red seal. Her lips part. Again we expect it: *eat*. Instead she stands with her back against the table. "Girls," she says, and she does not mean *women*, "thank you for your participation."

Years later a student enters my office and drops a paper on my desk. Before I glance at it, she rolls up her sleeves. Outside, it is raining; the light in my office is pewter-blue. Through the gloom, I notice that her arms are covered with bracelets. As my vision adjusts, I realize they are scars.

Her name is sweet; her hands are graceful. In the faint light we look at each other and do not say a word. We do not need to; we speak the way women have always spoken to each other. My face tells her I will remember; her body tells me she trusts nobody.

When she leaves, her inked-up paper clutched so tight I know her scars must sting, I bend my head to my book again. I try to bring myself back, back to language, back to the words that will make her tale untrue. I try to read my way out of what I've seen, but the letters won't let me. Late late nights and early mornings I write, trying desperately to communicate without using my body, sick of knowing only that one language, the language of flesh and blood and pain. I want access to the words men use. I want in, into the club, where the light is strong and arms can carry someone. I want to enter. And I realize that I have known this from the beginning.

Glory Sue's lips part again.

"Touch yourselves."

We look down, at our red shoes.

"Touch yourselves." She puts her hands on her waist. "I want you to feel how fat food has made you. *This*," and she pinches her flesh until her fingers are full, "is cake. *This* is pie. Feel it. Feel your fatness. Feel how much of yourself you would like to slice off."

At first we're shy We aren't used to our own skin. Mine feels flaky, dry, crusted. Beside me, Tara gnaws on her thumb. But soon someone puts a hand on her upper arm.

"I hate this," she says. "How it jiggles. I wish I could cut it off."

We begin to move.

Jasmine puts one hand on her hips; someone else cups her breasts in both hands and bends forward. I touch my nose. Tara puts both hands on her legs; I see her in the mirror. I watch as she runs both hands up and down her thighs, over and over. Soon I follow, imitating her, running my hands up and down my thighs, over and over, along with her, dispossessing my flesh. We touch ourselves, cutting our limbs in half, winnowing and winnowing, and it feels, even now, describing it, like bloody handprints marking every inch wretched.

I see Tara in the mirror, undoing herself. She is watching her own hands, her own eyes. But in the midst of our feast, her gaze meets mine. We stare at each other in the glass, we stare, and the cutting, the severing, the slicing and winnowing become something else. I watch her watch me, my hands on my thighs, and I watch her hands reply, parting her lips.

It will be years before I can name the something else in her eyes, before a woman names the something else in mine. It will be years before I can name it, desire; years before a woman bleeds into my hands and I think *yes yes* this is what blood is for, salt and not cotton, *yes yes* this and not children, *yes yes* and *please*. It will be years before I learn to scream, before my name matches the mirror, before the words I speak spell something besides *rape* and the foods I eat become poetry; it will be years before I name the difference, name it *desire*, name it *anger*, name it after a color women feel but cannot see.

On Carnival Lights, Compression, and Mice

My father loved mice, but he also loved me. What I understood of his vocation was a room like my childhood bedroom, filled floor to ceiling with books and baby animals in cages. I don't remember how I came to understand that the mice my father studied were injected with disease. But on the occasion of a dinner party for his colleagues, my pet mice disappeared.

"It's a secret," I told my mother, refusing to divulge their whereabouts. "Don't tell Daddy's friends or they might steal my mice and make them sick."

Childhood was a world of fine lines, careful distinctions. My father and I had mice, but they weren't the same mice. My father had cartoon characters, but their seriousness was never in doubt. There was a t-shirt emblazoned with a giant chicken, the words "POX BUSTERS" printed below. It looked like the t-shirts I wore in grade school, but represented his work on the chickenpox vaccine. As I grew older I stole his sweaters and tattered corduroys. I stole his gestures, so in photographs we are sitting at the same angle, our arms and legs crossed the exact same way. As a girl, I wanted to emulate my mother— the model, the gifted hostess—but that veneer always wore off, revealing the awkward introvert beneath.

My father the scientist had an uncanny ability to move toward a fixed point—the beautiful solution—with blinders on. He moved with speed, ambitious in the best sense, meaning ethical, driven by both curiosity and empathy. He moved undeterred by distractions around him. And if by distractions I mean me, I also mean corruption and cruelty, pettiness and bureaucracy. He had integrity, my father, and street geek style. He arrived at meetings in mismatched socks, threadbare sneakers, and corduroys he'd purchased in high school. He often ate family dinners standing up. He had eaten standing up in the Navy and the habit stuck, plus it allowed him to read.

My father the mathematician moved unswerved toward the elegant answer, toward numbers so bright in the distance that he forgot to look both ways for cars.

"You must," said my mother once, "look both ways for him when he crosses the street."

And so I became Janus, their New Year's baby, a good girl with one bad girl foot off the curb.

❖

My father's work in science and math is often described by his peers as elegant. Often that's the one aspect of his work that I can understand. It wasn't for lack of trying that I did poorly in math and science. No matter how many hours he spent helping me with my homework, I couldn't separate numbers from the fingers I used to count, or stop terminology from sliding, words losing meaning as they rolled toward music.

After years spent trying to choose between conflicting interests, between the elegant abstractions of math and the inelegant but ethically-motivated drive to heal humankind, my father reconciled them in epidemiology, which allowed him to live in the beautiful, poised world of numbers while striving, still, to heal the sick. To cure the flesh without touching the flesh—to tell the story without telling a story—to express emotion without actually feeling—my father wanted the essence of the thing without the dirt. He wanted the view from a window, a smooth pane of glass between the world and his gaze.

❖

My father was prolific in each of the fields he entered, writing articles that engaged with, and often generated, the questions of his day. But he did not write books. Books are rare in his field, a field where speed and wide distribution are necessary for advancement.

"Medicine," he said, "doesn't wait for the book."

Because he and his peers did not write books, they had

a fascination with, and maybe envy of, writers who produced them. My father spoke with bewilderment and awe of a colleague who had published several books. When I pointed out that his books weren't serious—weren't groundbreaking and intellectually challenging like my father's articles—my father shrugged.

"But Cal, they're books. You can hold them, set them on the table. You can wrap them in paper and give them as gifts."

When at last my father co-edited a book, he and I both found it funny that the subject of the book was placebos. For years my father and I had engaged in a running joke about medical conference souvenirs, each of us trying to outdo the other by thinking up garish, inappropriate themes for tote bags and mugs. The joke began when my father arrived home from a conference on prostate cancer bearing an enormous coffee mug embossed with a multi-colored image of an oversized prostate.

My mother was horrified, and begged him to get rid of it. I saved it from the garbage that day, and from then on my father delighted in bringing me the most ridiculous freebies he could find. My favorite was a gold pen with "VIAGRA" printed in bold letters, which I use in faculty meetings when I'm having a tough day.

"You're lucky I didn't get you a luggage tag," he told me. "The stats on stealing luggage with Viagra tags are pretty high."

When *The Science of the Placebo* was published, my father joked about what sorts of freebies might accompany its distribution.

"How about a coffee mug without a bottom?"

"How about pens with invisible ink?"

My father was proud of his book, although he never said so. Pride was high on his list of sins. I could tell only because he gave me not one but two copies of *The Science of the Placebo*. The book is hot pink, and I'll admit the cover is not the most attractive thing about it. It has two profiles juxtaposed on the front, presumably to suggest the notion of ghosting that placebos embody. Inside, the articles tend to the topic of medical ethics with seriousness, but also grace. I sense my father's presence as an editor simply because I can actually read the articles and make sense of them. My father hated jargon. He loved simplicity in language: clarity, compression. He co-edited this volume with a Kleinman, a Kusek, and an Engel, and I wonder if they shared, not only his integrity about the ethics of scientific inquiry, but his obsession with clarity and compression, as well. Sometimes when I miss my father I am tempted to try to talk to Kleinman, Kusek, and/or Engel, to ask them for anecdotes, odd little bits about his character. Instead I open the book at random and find words I like: "deceptive administration," "voodoo death," "equipoise." My father would have liked these words, too, and we'd have punned around with them, creating new meanings.

⁕

I inherited both my father's introverted nature and his obsession with the aesthetics of compression. They seem related, concerned with shutting things out. It gives me great pleasure to pare sentences down, to make stories smaller, more private, contained. I feel so much, too much most days. I prefer being alone to almost anyone's company. The world is a great carnival of flashing lights, whip cracks, and popcorn smells that trail me home, stuck to the hem of my skirt.

When I write, and especially when I revise to make things tiny and perfect, I make amends for my introversion and awkwardness. I am forgiven my unwillingness to socialize. When I write, I take the overwhelming world and winnow it into a window, from which I can see you, but you can't see me.

Of course, there is no craft without content. There is no relation to compression without a relation to release. Compression is the opposite of excess, which means that an emphasis on compression's precision, perfectionism, and delicacy is haunted by traces of its reckless, garrulous, sexy sibling.

Compression, meet Passion.
But that is an essay for another time.

TWO

Of Quarterbacks and Quarantine

A Brief History of Quarantine

The word quarantine derives from the Italian word *quaranta*, meaning forty, or the number of days land travelers were isolated to prevent the spread of disease in the fourteenth century seaport city of Ragusa. These days, it's useful to draw a distinction between the concept of quarantine and the concept of isolation. The latter refers to the separation and confinement of those known to carry a contagion; the former refers to the same treatment used on those simply suspected of being contagious.

I start with the concept of quarantine because isolation has been central to my experience as an out lesbian professor at a small, regional American university. In graduate school, I studied with several lesbian professors; they were out, professionally and socially, but in relying heavily on poststructuralist theory, they de-emphasized specifically lesbian and gay texts. Their courses centered on broad categories like "sexuality and narrative" and "feminism and psychoanalysis." In some instances, their excitement about theory was inspiring. In other instances, they hid behind the texts, avoiding the challenge of acknowledging queer students and changing campus climate.

Acting as if you're post-gay is fine when you went to Berkeley and you're teaching at a research one; acting as if you're post-gay when you've just been hired as the first out lesbian ever to teach at a small Christian college in Nebraska is a good way to get killed. I was gay-bashed and received death threats my first year in a tenure-track position in Nebraska. Yet while I received death threats for being so out, several of my students never realized I was a lesbian. It took years to understand that different geographies require different political strategies, and that each classroom demands a tailored approach.

By the time I arrived at my current job over a decade ago, I was traumatized. I don't use that word lightly: I thought I might die in Nebraska, or that one of my queer students or allies might be murdered. Having moved from a playfully post-gay environment to the terrain of violent homophobia, on my current job I entered a third, equally unfamiliar realm.

I'm grateful to say that many of my colleagues are wonderfully open-minded, progressive intellectuals whose personal and academic accomplishments challenge me to be a better teacher. I count myself lucky to work with these folks. There are staff members and administrators on campus whose integrity I seek to emulate, and whose compassion for students is obvious in everything they do. There are also a few other out queer faculty and staff who are trying very hard to address the campus climate. I don't want to downplay the positive aspects of a job I love, and wouldn't dream of leaving.

Overall, however, the campus climate I've experienced for the past decade is chilly, detached. Visible hatred is rare, but I'm often ostracized from conversations and social events. Ignorance about queer issues is still treated as a healthy norm. In this climate, I've been asked such questions as "Are straight students allowed to take your classes?" and "I don't come out to my students as heterosexual; why do you need to tell your students you're gay?" During a discussion about spousal hires (my department currently has four), I was accused of discriminating against straight people when I observed that this practice is tied to the heterosexual privilege of marriage. At a book signing in the campus bookstore, a colleague picked up my most recent poetry collection, read the back cover copy, and made a cruel homophobic remark to my face. While preparing my tenure file, I was even asked if the jagged edges escaping my otherwise pristine binder were deliberate:

"Did you do that on purpose?"
"No, the department hole punch doesn't work very well."
"I thought perhaps you were making a statement. You know—about being different and all."

Worst of all is a kind of casual shunning, rendering me invisible. Some might call hallway banter unimportant, but hallways are classrooms, too. Faculty meetings, committees, the campus gym, faculty lounges, bathrooms, and parking lots are our classrooms, the spaces where faculty learn invisible, unspoken aspects of professional behavior.

Given the chilly climate, and in spite of my professional accomplishments, it's not always clear to me how I was hired in the first place, but I suspect that my feminine appearance and race privilege were instrumental in declaring me a fit. Would I have been hired if I was a butch dyke or a transman/transwoman who didn't pass? Would I have been hired if I was a person of color? I recall one job candidate, a strong woman who looked awkward in her ill-fitting skirt. She wasn't out as queer, but her gender identity was visible. Discussions about her interview centered on her aggressive answers to our questions, on her lack of warmth, on her awkward demeanor. In the end, she was passed over for a woman with a wedding ring who talked quite a bit about her husband. Another interview, with an Asian-American gay man, went equally badly when several of my colleagues reacted to his slightly feminine demeanor, dismissing him as flamboyant and dramatic. His gender identity and his race disturbed their notions of what a professor should be.

Many of my fellow queer writers labor as sex toy salesclerks, strippers, rent boys, and pornographers. They talk a politics I share and live a politics I don't. I'm privileged, yes, and live outside their center, the urban core at the heart of their texts. I feel stuffy and stern in this setting. Simply having health insurance differentiates me from many of my friends. Yet I feel unkempt at school, where my insistence on the political and experiential aspect of what I study is off-putting to some of my Ivory Tower peers.

I'm in my forties now; like other queers my age or older, I knew I was a lesbian long before I'd ever met another lesbian, or even seen one on TV. Nobody in my world was out; my understanding of the concept of queerness was rooted in blatant homophobia. So vast was the split between my sense of myself as a good person and my understanding of queer people as inherently evil and immoral that I hid what I knew about myself and developed a double life. I lived this way until I was twenty-one. Then I began the long, arduous process of unlearning my own ignorance, and trying to create a life in which my sense of self and my public identity could be reconciled.

Questions and Celebrations

I began teaching at twenty-two. In many ways my professional development as a teacher paralleled my personal development as a lesbian. Stepping into a classroom in my late twenties as a tenure-track professor, I had no idea that this process was unfinished, or that I needed to finish it. I thought of myself as well-adjusted; my teaching and writing careers were successful, although my early relationships were not.

So on my first day of teaching GLBT Studies, I was baffled to find myself unable to speak the words "gay, lesbian, bisexual, and transgender" in front of the class. Stack of syllabi in hand, I criss-crossed the rows of desks, smiling an anxious, fake smile and handing a syllabus to each student. Then I called roll. With seventy-five students, this takes a while. Still we had time on our hands, so I faced them. I needed to talk. I don't remember what I said.

My panic surprised me. I'd been out to everyone in my life for nearly a decade and had published several books on queer topics. It took much of that school year for me to realize the extent to which I'd downplayed aspects of my lesbian identity so as not to offend others. That year, I learned the difference between being out and being visible. In a classroom situation where I needed to speak openly about GLBT issues I froze, feeling shame and stigma I hadn't expected. Yet here was a room full of students expecting me to unravel the origins of that shame and stigma, to move beyond it, to teach them things about queer literature, history, philosophy, and culture.

A significant number of students dropped the class after that first disastrous meeting. Since then, I'm pleased to say that I often over-enroll the class, adding four or five students who beg to take it, claiming it will change their lives. I believe them; it's certainly changed mine.

The context of teaching my first GLBT Studies class amazes me when I think back on it. First and foremost, I was teaching a class I knew nothing about. My qualifications for the class were largely personal; I knew very little about GLBT history or literature beyond my own interests. I'd read tons of poststructuralist theory in graduate school, but the emphasis in my program was narrowly focused on Judith Butler's dismantling of identity. The latter, I soon learned, did not make a good starting point for teaching GLBT Studies at a small university in a suburban town surrounded by conservative farming communities. Students had signed up for one of the only classes in which we were going to talk about gay people, and here I was saying they didn't exist. I had to learn to set the literature in context—poststructuralist theory, sure, but first capitalism, WWI and WWII, the Civil Rights Movement, second-wave feminism, HIV/AIDS, the War on Terror, and many other factors that shape how Americans today conceptualize sexual identity, sex, and gender. Once I began organizing the class around general paradigms and historical shifts, things got easier. Butler's arguments made sense, instead of nonsense, and students learned that they could pick and choose an intellectual approach to what is, in fact, a hopelessly broad topic.

Looking back, I understand that my expectations for the class were shamefully low. I anticipated all manner of resistance, and envisioned class as a nonstop battle. I thought haters would sign up for the class just to heckle me, and that the few visible queer students would radiate shame.

What happened was in fact the opposite. From day one the class was excited about the material. Most of the students who signed up were genuinely interested, whether because they knew someone queer, were queer themselves, or simply grasped that this topic was central to contemporary American political and cultural history.

One of the unexpected challenges of teaching Queer Studies is that instead of fighting against resistance, I sometimes have to generate it in order for discussion to be productive. As my syllabus states: our aim is to question, rather than simply celebrate, the identities gay, lesbian, bisexual, and transgender.

Another challenge is breaking down barriers between our class and the university. My students are very good at this; I try to follow their lead. One of my students recently raised hell in a "Women and Literature" class where the instructor refused to allow any lesbian representations whatsoever, claiming they didn't belong on the syllabus. Students have formed groups to push for more gender-neutral bathrooms on campus and for GLBT friendly housing in the dorms. They've started groups like Brown Pride, a group focusing on the lives of GLBT people of color, and groups for transgender people and allies.

Perhaps the most unexpected challenge comes from the few students in class who openly identify as queer. They are often my strongest critics, dissatisfied when the course doesn't cover every topic. One year, a number of students identifying as bisexual became increasingly angry with me, with the class, with the world. No representation of bisexuality that I chose for class discussion was good enough; I was biphobic, and that was that. This tends to happen every year, but with a different identity category or event stirring up strong feelings. I listen and learn; I examine my teaching practices and prejudices, but at the end of the day, I also have to let some of it go. I can't be everything to all of them, and they want that, especially the queer students. I do, however, let them know that I'm available to talk, and they crowd my office during office hours.

One teaching method that works especially well for this class is the response essay. Students write five short response essays over the course of the quarter; I grade them pass/fail. The purpose of pass/fail grading is twofold: with seventy-five students in class, five essays each, and a major research paper at the end of the ten week quarter, I'd be overwhelmed if I made copious comments on each response essay. But it's also a great way to find out what students are really thinking. I promise they can write anything they'd like, and I won't pass judgment. I won't fail them based on content, even if that content is angry or disdainful of the material. No question is stupid; no observation is ignorant. The only rules are that the essays must be academic (not personal), and that they must focus on readings and/or class discussions.

In this context, students write honestly about their confusion, fears, and beliefs. I learn who's quiet because they're freaked out and who's quiet because they're shy. I get glimpses of why they're taking the class and what I need to do differently. The essays are often moving; they're also often surprisingly funny. Occasionally a student's essay is a cry for help, and I respond by meeting with them personally, expressing my concern, and directing them to the appropriate services.

As a writer, I use the class as an opportunity to develop new audiences for experimental literature, independent presses, and living writers. A canon of GLBT texts is forming; books like *The Well of Loneliness* and *Becoming a Man* are examples of texts every scholar should someday read. However, I prefer to bring in texts students might not find on their own. In recent years I've taught Richard Siken's *Crush* and Carl Phillips' *The Rest of Love*; I often teach Rebecca Brown, Carole Maso, and Eileen Myles rather than Sarah Waters or Jeanette Winterson. For small presses like RedBone Press or Steel Toe Books, an order of 75 texts is a substantial financial boost. My students and I talk about this: not only what we're reading, but who publishes it, and why. Whenever possible, I bring in local queer writers and direct students to readings at our town's fabulous independent bookstore. In this way I connect the class to my other specialty, Creative Writing; in this way I generate new audiences for independent publishing.

Often, the classroom feels like an oasis from the

heterosexism and homophobia I experience among my peers. As my students strive to learn what I'm teaching, I strive to achieve the level of comfort they feel with their identities. My bond with them is often deeper than the tenuous or nonexistent bonds I experience with my colleagues.

The Quarterback and the Magnetic Bear

One year several members of our college football team enrolled in my class. Perhaps a homophobic remark prompted coaches to suggest it; perhaps it simply fit their training schedules. Whatever the reason, they were reluctant participants.

Mid-quarter everything changed when a group of openly gay young men decided to infiltrate the football squad's position on the classroom field during small group discussion. Four gay men strolled over to the football players, who'd made a circle with their chairs. Dead silence. Then a cheerful voice: "Let's start on page twelve."

The beauty of the moment was evident to me. Here were young gay men who'd perhaps had a painful relation to institutionalized sports in high school. For once, they had the power. They were smart on this subject, and they had knowledge the football players needed. I don't mean lived experience (although that, too); I mean interest and tenacity. The readings were difficult, but they were prepared. They knew I'd maintain order, and they knew that teasing was out of the question.

I avoided the group, letting them work it out for themselves. By the end of class something had changed. I won't say the football team looked thrilled to be there, but there were a few smiles and inquisitive expressions on the faces of the football players. I stopped by the group to ask how it was going.

"I feel a little weird," said Jeff, one of the football players. "I've never really talked to gay people before."

If there's a secret to my method of teaching this class,

the secret lies in making space for the word "weird." Rather than disowning or criticizing students' discomfort with the material, with me, with each other, I make room for it, even when students say things that make me cringe inwardly. The class can't be about mandating approval or demanding that students agree with me, each other, or any given text. For the most part, they come to trust this, and to voice their fears, anxiety, and discomfort openly.

When I teach this course during winter quarter, one assignment centers on Valentine's Day, and the distinction between homophobia and heterosexism. Much Valentine's Day rhetoric isn't homophobic, but it is heterosexist. Conveying to students just how prevalent heterosexist ideologies are can be difficult. Valentine's Day makes it easy, so I send students off campus to find examples of heterosexist rhetoric in town, on TV, etc.

Our class met the day after Valentine's, and I asked everyone to write down the examples they'd found.

To my surprise, the first student to raise a hand was Jeff. He explained that he and his girlfriend had visited a store for Valentine's Day. He wanted to buy her something she'd like, and she picked out two little magnetic bears, his and hers.

"Then I remembered the assignment," Jeff said. He wanted to see if same-sex bear couples would stick together magnetically, too. But when he and his girlfriend tried it, the magnets didn't work.

"Magnetic bears are heterosexist!" he said. "It made us mad. So I got her something else for Valentine's Day."

The whole class was quiet. I really wanted to laugh and I really wanted to cry and I felt exceedingly happy.

"That's smart and interesting, Jeff. What a good example," and of course, it was. Then the class jumped to praise him, and I could see on Jeff's face that this experience—of being called smart, of speaking aloud in class, of participating in an intellectual sphere—was new and exciting.

This was what I hadn't understood, hadn't expected: I

was not alone on my quarantine island. Although isolated by and from my colleagues, I was quarantined with my students. This bonding, this shared sense of community, surprised and delighted me. It delights me still.

Note

Gensini, Gian Franco, Magdi H. Yacoub, Andrea A. Conti. 'The concept of quarantine in history: from plague to SARS.' *Journal of Infection* (2004) 49, 257–261.

Reading and Teaching *The Terrible Girls*

Some time ago, in response to a lecture on Rebecca Brown's novel *The Dogs*, a student posed a puzzling question. *The Dogs* describes a female protagonist whose studio apartment is occupied by a pack of unruly, violent dogs.

"Why didn't the narrator just send the dogs to the Humane Society?"

At first I thought my student was joking, but no. Her dogs were real; they had to be. As a reader, she was a Fundamentalist. The author wrote dogs, and dogs came to be.

This misrecognition of metaphor is the place I begin when I teach Brown's work. I use her texts regularly in "Introduction to GLBT Literature," a course that enrolls seventy-five college freshmen and sophomores each year. We start with imagination and creativity, with the difference between creative writing and criticism. We talk about how frightening it can be to read a text with multiple meanings, and how to decide which meanings read best. We talk about pleasure: how curiosity and mystery coexist, and how gaps and erasures contribute to meaning. Brown's dogs switch codes, shapes, and genres. My students understand this as serious play, particularly in "The Big Queer Class" my colleagues refer to as "Literature of Historically Marginalized Groups."

I teach Brown's *The Terrible Girls* less frequently than *The Dogs*, *The Gifts Of The Body*, or *Excerpts from a Family Medical Dictionary*. Sometimes I have to protect myself from my students, from their uglier misreadings and casual dismissals. I am protective of *The Terrible Girls*. Brown's approach to familiar lesbian literary tropes feels wholly original here. Certainly the book startled me when I first read it. Here was the image of the closeted lesbian lover; here self-sacrifice; here invisibility; here conflicts between politics and passion. Yet none of these things existed strictly on a realist level. They were coded, not in the subtle language used by pre-Stonewall writers, but in vivid metaphors and magical realism. The code wasn't written to protect the writer, but to engage the reader. The code was a device meant to outlast whatever conditions might alter later literary approaches to same-sex desire.

Take away the closet in Radclyffe Hall's *The Well Of Loneliness*, and there's no story. Take away the closet in *The Terrible Girls*, and you still have the pain of a lover's betrayal, the misuse of power that comes with privilege. When I read *The Terrible Girls* I see my lesbian history, but it's possible to read the book without engaging its queerness. While such a reading isn't preferable or honest, it speaks to the significance of the book's themes, and their applicability to any human relationship. The book endures misreadings in generous fashion.

In the opening chapter, "The Dark House," the protagonist serves her lover coffee at a conference. Disguised as a maid, she sacrifices visibility, allowing her lover to dismiss not only their relationship, but all similar relationships. As the protagonist states, "You had made me the coffee-cart girl." I gasped when I first read that line, both because it's a great and memorable line, and because it broke a tacit rule that had long burdened my writing. As Sarah Schulman notes, "in what appears to me to be an attempt to manufacture, rather than reflect lesbian culture, like the Stalinists we have developed a sort of lesbian Socialist Realism which has come to dominate lesbian fiction." How liberating to come across Brown's work, where poetic language takes priority over crippling political correctness, and where gothic imagery elevates metaphor to the level of spiritual iconography.

Years after first reading *The Terrible Girls*, I came across Richard Siken's poetry collection *Crush*. Again I felt the thrill of gratitude for a queer writer who dared turn a critical eye on himself and his lovers. The best queer writing does this, I think. There's *Cool For You*, Eileen Myles's brilliant nonfiction novel; there's *Notice*, Heather Lewis's masterpiece of self-deception. Something in me longs for queer voices that dare admit our own guilt and responsibility; not because I don't see how the world damages us (and how the world damages us!), but because I am easily bored. Yes, homophobia nearly killed me; yes, it has damaged or even killed many of my friends and lovers. Yet as an artist, I can only say that so many times. At some point what's between us is between us, and if we ruin it, we must bear witness.

The Terrible Girls doesn't answer the questions it asks, but it asks the right questions. Like the speaker in Adrienne Rich's "Twenty-One Love Poems," Brown's protagonist wonders whether lesbians are partly responsible if we allow the outside world to distort our relationships. The self-sacrificing protagonist in *The Terrible Girls* was damaged before she met her lover, but that isn't Brown's focus. Her focus lies in the present of the protagonist's life, in the sacrifice of her right arm:

> We kept my arm in the bathtub, bleeding like a fish. When I went to bed, the water was the color of rose water, with thick red lines like strings. And when I woke up the first time to change my bandages, it was colored like salmon. Then it was carnation red, and then maroon, then burgundy, then purple, thick, and almost black by morning.

Here and elsewhere, Brown substitutes sound and imagery for narrative logic, evoking Gertrude Stein's pleasure in word play and musical repetition. Yet Brown's obsession with lying and truth-telling also links linguistic pleasure to betrayal: "language is the only thing that lies." What a burden for a writer; what a gift. If language lies, we are all creative writers. Our stories are never true, our metaphors always fabulous. Our dogs are dogs, then ghosts, then cities, then lovers who fail to fall back into bed.

When I challenge students to imitate a writer we've studied, Brown is often their first choice. Their narrators unburden themselves of gravity, falling into crooked arms. What stays with me is the voice of a protagonist addressing her lover without concern for what the world thinks. Direct address, rage coupled with passion, violent imagery that may or may not be literal: I see these things in contemporary writers, and think of a lineage that includes Stein, Woolf, Plath, and Brown.

I don't remember what I told my student about *The Dogs and the Humane Society*, but I remember her puzzlement turning to relief. It's a relief to free oneself of narrow-mindedness. It's the burden of the queer female writer to escape both the straitjacket of political correctness and the spangled bodice of Romance. Reading Brown's work did this for me.

Note

Rebecca Brown, *The Terrible Girls*, City Lights Publishers, 2001.

Sarah Schulman, 'Is Lesbian Culture Only for Beginners?' *My American History: Lesbian and Gay Life During the Reagan/Bush Years*, Routledge, 1994.

Suspect

Heather Lewis's second novel, *Notice*, is a work of genius. Underrated, rarely discussed, the book belongs with contemporary classics. It is perhaps the most disturbing book I've ever read, and among the most compelling. It illuminates the state of female, specifically lesbian, subjectivity under contemporary American regimes by deconstructing genres that have failed to capture women's experiences: pulp, noir, mystery, romance. It subverts these genres, yet never falls prey to the directives of political correctness.

Notice was published posthumously. Its narrative voice was so unique that no press would touch it until Lewis committed suicide at 40. Her suicide allowed the book's publication; now she was dead, and sufficiently chastened for examining experiences that mainstream culture attempts to suppress.

Before she killed herself, Lewis wrote one more novel, *The Second Suspect*. This book was published and reviewed during her lifetime. It was bought and it was read.

The Second Suspect is a terrible book. But it's not just a bad book; it's so much more. It's a bad book riffing off the author's masterpiece. *The Second Suspect* is a rewriting of *Notice*, but minus everything that makes *Notice* literary. *The Second Suspect* takes plot, characters, and themes from *Notice* and reduces them to formulaic drivel.

The Second Suspect is the work of an author who understood that her masterpiece had been censored, tossed aside, misunderstood. So she sat down and rewrote it. She made it bad, deliberately bad. And the public loved it.

Thoughts on Prose Blocks
as Dance and Resistance

Writing this, looking out this particular window at a paper mill and a parking garage, I'm not married. I was married once, and I'm not divorced, but neither am I married at this moment. It's a puzzle, isn't it? The pieces don't fit. To find the answer you must cross the border.

Take a right from my house. Turn left at the light. Take the long low road until it hits the highway. Take the highway across the Canadian border. Here, in Vancouver, I'm married again.

In Vancouver, my love and I are bound together. In Seattle, we're severed; not even annulled, simply disappeared. Which is to say that the stakes in naming are high. To name a thing is to allow it entry into your world. To refuse to name it means to refuse to see it; or, subversively, to refuse to acquiesce to interpellation.

Start again: It's possible for me to tell a different kind of story about prose poetry. To describe the constant tension I experience between the impulse to make meaning and the impulse to focus on sound alone, on letters as musical notation. In this story I don't know what I'm looking for, but when I find it, my heart beats faster. In this story the two novels that were my first books feel far away; I can't find enough uninterrupted space to complete another novel. After a decade of teaching full-time, beaten down by all that comes with the struggle for tenure, I decide to stop. Stop trying to squeeze my life into a form that doesn't fit. I decide to abandon traditional forms and squeeze everything—unfinished novels, stories, essays, poems, fragments—into tiny, tight blocks. Compression creates an unexpectedly playful, pleasurable process. What's unsaid matters as much as what's said. By narrowing my vision I've created a different kind of beauty. Because I'm working in such small spaces, I have enough time to make each line musical. That music matters more to me now than stretching time across the page.

It makes sense, then—this movement from novels to prose blocks. But how to explain why I'm not using line breaks, white space, fragments as often as I did in my first book of poetry? That's harder to explain, even to myself. I think it has to do with wanting to create a specific sort of sound. This, too, ties back to place. When I moved to the Pacific Northwest from the East Coast, Deep South, Great Plains, and Midwest, I was entranced by the music I found here—Sleater-Kinney, Elliott Smith, Laura Veirs, The Gossip. A DIY aesthetic links these sounds, but there's something else, too. A long breath, exhaled. I think of New York City as a gasp. The South was held in, and the Great Plains, hardened. I want to write sentences that involve the body: lots of falling, a curved spine, propulsion. A prose block is dance; it's also a compressed novel (a novel the writer doesn't have time to write) and a rogue lyric (a song the writer hopes will never end).

THREE

Girl of Yes, and An End to Highways

The air in this town smells like cantaloupe and the high school looks like a prison. There's a punishment light halfway down Elm. Bellingham's resident white supremacist, a balding man in a 70s track suit, jogs across town every morning carrying his breakfast in a paper bag. Railroad Avenue is downtown Bellingham, Washington's main drag, a once elegant strip of turn-of-the-century buildings. There's an herbal remedy shop run by a woman who grows her own herbs; she'll diagnose all your ills from one strand of your hair. There's a pawn shop filled with guns and guitars, and AA meetings in the Hotel Helena. The sex offender's playground looks down from the top of the hill, over a city built on gold digging and gambling, prostitution and Empire. Native American names hover over the town on truck stops and casino marquees.

Every other store on Railroad Avenue looks like a drug front. A few blocks up on State Street one of the restaurants boasts a handprinted sign: Closed for Vacation. The vacation has lasted a year so far. One of my friends, a bartender, says she's been asked for Oxycontin, meth, heroin, and crack all in the same night. Once a frustrated customer opened a bag of coke and dumped it in her hair. The restaurant where she mixed margaritas recently got busted. It boasts shuttered windows and padlocked doors. Just beyond the padlock is a newly swept, newly empty storefront. Taped to the inner glass are glossy plans to turn the block-length building into pricey condos.

Corporate coffee recently moved onto the corner of Railroad and Holly, into a glossy new building Bellingham locals can't get used to. The broken windows are surely accidents, stray bottles meant to be tossed into the two story hole that lived on the corner long before developers filled it with condos. Back then the hole was occupied by squatters who strung hammocks and slept in the air, set fires and cooked on the ground below. They set up elaborate sewage systems and had friends drop supplies down on pulleys, into the space they called Pit Park. Over time the park was filled with tents and gardens. At night you could climb down a rope ladder and sit around a barrel fire, listening to air guitar. The police raid that ended it all was followed by a ribbon-cutting ceremony. One of the squatters erected a blowup doll with a lipstick sign that read Don't inflate the 'Ham.

This is the City of Subdued Excitement, where vets cluster in yurts, inching closer and closer to Canada. Sunlight happens three months a year. This is a city where art and violence have the same velocity, where someone's knitting sweaters for the skinniest trees: black and white stripes, pink buttons crawling up the bark.

⁂

Elizabeth and I met in this mill town, this sweaters-for-trees town. We fell in love walking the ledge to the logjam, eyeing the teeth of the cold, clear stream. We tucked up our pantlegs and took off our shoes, draped our socks among the trees. We tucked our sleeves into our sleeves, turned cartwheels in the warm, wet sand.

For many years I feared I wasn't made for love, just a fierce and reckless solitude marked on my body: the cruel pink scar that flowers, strange dahlia, on my left shoulder.

"Your scar," Elizabeth began, that day at the logjam. "You've got one on your back, too. An identical flower."

Two marks, not just one as I'd always believed. Might I—maybe—please—pretty—be marked for the galaxy of a lover's gaze?

First kiss came to shut me up.

My cherry print scarf dipped into the bay.

⁂

Years after that day we dance in our kitchen. Elizabeth swings her right hand in a windmill. I shake my hips and move my arms side-to-side.

She calls my geeky dance move "Shaking the Baby."

"I look ridiculous."

"Yes, you do."

We dance to Snoop Dogg and Sleater-Kinney. "They go together," she says, and I'm not sure which unlikely pair she means: S-K and Snoop, my blind dog and her twenty-two pound cat, her windmill and my awkward gestures.

Our mismatched family, our commingling.

❖

This is a city of farmers and farmland, outdoor markets and companion llamas. On one of our visits to the farmer's market we're stopped in our tracks.

"Would you like to buy a bridge?"

I spent my 20s in New York. I know this trick.

Elizabeth spent her 20s in Georgia. She says yes, and buys a brick.

The bridge seller is a farmer; the salvaged bridge and bricks are soon to be part of a building housing the farmer's market all year round. So it's legitimate, this brick. And the bridge, too—an actual bridge saved from destruction by Bellingham's garbage company. The indoor farmer's market will bridge the community, connecting consumers to farmers, a cornerstone of slow food.

Elizabeth purchases a tiny part of this building, a single brick with our names etched in. When the bricks are planted we spend half an hour searching until we discover we're standing on top of our names.

❖

I would dye, I say, these things blue for you:
my ex-lover's shirt
my city's gray sky

❖

Sometimes we walk to Boulevard Park, a grassy promenade bordering Bellingham Bay. We look for our history here, reading between the lines on the wooden sign suspended above the view: Bellingham Bay was claimed by Captain George Vancouver in 1792, and named for a Naval Officer, Sir William Bellingham. This coastal Washington city appears to have been colonized by British fags. Our history, the history of colonialism disguised as discovery. Our history, the history of lovers disguised as friends.

❖

This is the city where we wish to marry. But in July 2006, after months of debating, the Washington State Supreme Court rules 5-4 against same-sex marriage, upholding the state's Defense of Marriage Act. For weeks in the press we read about "the sanctity of marriage," and listen as our fellow citizens compare same-sex affection to bestiality and necrophilia.

In defiance, I venture to the jewelry store downtown to stare at displays of "His and Hers" rings. Finally I work up the nerve to make a purchase.

"Two plain silver bands, both size six, thank you."

"Your husband," she says, "must have very small hands."

❖

In the end we cross the border, small hands and all, in search of a country that will allow us to marry. Canada is just thirty minutes away; we skim the highway from Bellingham to B.C. On our first trip, we procure the license; the notary crosses out "groom" and writes "Bride #2." Some weeks later we return for our wedding, accompanied by friends to witness our vows. Traffic lights love us. Red turns glitter-green. We drive the bustling streets of Vancouver in search of the stranger who will deliver our vows.

We found her on the internet, this stranger who will marry us in her apartment. She's beautiful, red hair turning silver, and her vows make us weep. It's as easy as stealing plastic forks from a coffee shop down the street, easy as paper plates the red-haired woman won't let us use, insisting we use her elegant china. We can barely cut the cake, it's such thick chocolate. We can't believe we've said it, "love," in the presence of strangers. Our witnesses watch us, as if to know how.

After the ceremony we stumble into a convenience store to pick up toothpaste. We're married, two of us, all of us in love. We're women, tall and small, dark and light, black hair and blonde. Leigh Ann and Amy hold hands and read magazines. I scan for toothpaste, Elizabeth searches for gum. So we're separated for the first time all day when a woman with meth sores on her face stumbles into the store and the manager blocks her.

"Get out," he says. "I told you not to come in."

"I have money this time. I just want to eat."

"Get out," and he's on her, tackling her, and she fights back, and someone shouts, someone else gasps. She's on the floor. He's dragging her by her coat. More shouts, and a man runs into the store, grabs the manager's uniform, and slugs him. They brawl, the woman runs, grabbing sandwiches and soda. The man who punched the manager pulls a knife. Someone screams, and all I can do is watch Elizabeth across the room. We're waiting for the gun that must be next, for "lesbian romance ends in death." Leigh Ann and Amy stand flat to the walls. Sandwich girl is out the door, and knife man with her, the manager shouting after, and then we're all four through the doorway, shaking as we run for Amy's car. What does it mean, anyway? One minute you're one, the next minute you're two, the next minute a gunshot subtracts you again.

Dead tired, Elizabeth and I honeymoon in a high-rise hotel, dizzying ourselves with the drop from the window, taking photos of each other's shoulders, wrists, ankles, of our faces' new openness. Kiss. We go to sleep married and we wake from dreams married and we drink coffee married and then we drive home.

Our car looks small in the hubcap of the semi beside us. If someone erased us, there'd be room in traffic for one more car. The wheels pirouette, oblivious, toward the Peace Arch, where traffic stalls on the Canadian side. Our car inches forward. The obelisk approaches: the international boundary line between B.C. and WA.

Just before we cross into the U.S., Elizabeth takes a photograph of the two of us, our faces touching. Then, as the wheels roll over and the U.S. reclaims us, annulling our marriage, she takes another photo of the two of us together. Later we won't be able to tell the difference between the two shots.

Evelyn

Her name is Evelyn. She's lived in her house since 1960. She was born in 1915 or 1916, near the Nooksack River, which still floods its banks.

These are the facts.

This is the mystery: a 91-year-old woman and me. She can't hear me, but I talk with my hands.

Evelyn's surname is also a woman's name, old-fashioned and elegant. Her life in the past included a husband. Her hair was black. Our street was barren. The trees must've sprouted after she moved in. And the automobiles! Long, sexy, glistening.

❖

Our street is unusual because there is no alley. Out front is the park and out back, another street. In a town of alleyways this marks a distinction. We can see Evelyn's front porch from our backyard.

Not long after we moved in, I heard a scritch and looked across the backyard to someone's porch. The someone was an elderly someone, fragile, stooped nearly in half. She wore a bright red crocheted vest over a purple polyester shirt and beige polyester pants, with some brassy things for decoration. Her hair was silver, curled into ringlets. She opened the flap to her mailbox, then let it snap shut.

❖

For weeks I watched Evelyn water her hanging plant, hung too high by the door. Every morning her routine was the same. She placed a stepstool in front of the plant and set one foot on the stool. It wobbled, she wavered. She went back inside. Came out with a pot of water. Threw the water at the plant, streaking the side of her house with wet.

My first gift to Evelyn was a watering can: red plastic, shaped like an elephant.

❖

Evelyn's TV is always on. I don't know if she watches it, listens to it, or simply likes blur and fuzz for company. Maybe it was always on, and the husband who died never turned it off. Perhaps it was her life then, too.

One day I go over to her house and while we are sitting, not talking, my cell phone rings. I show her the generic pictures that fill the screen, pictures I don't have the technological savvy to replace. There's a puppy, a kitten, and an animated bear.

She stares at the puppy for a long time.

"My goodness." She grins. "Isn't that something?"

I want to show Evelyn the internet. Bring my laptop over, catch one of the inevitable open channels, and call up the web for her gaze. But I'm also afraid that if the old century meets the new, the sky will fall. This small town is "the city" to her. She's a farm girl. A girl born on the floodplain. A girl who rode horses and still curls her hair.

❖

One of my neighbors volunteers with the local historical society. When she learned that I knew Evelyn, she asked to meet her, to record her history. Susan followed me to Evelyn's house one afternoon and we knocked on the door. When Evelyn didn't answer, I climbed the back steps and tapped on her kitchen window. Susan looked horrified by my rogue knock, by the frail state of Evelyn's porch. This was not the sanitized version of elder lore she'd expected. When Evelyn finally answered, it only got worse.

"Who are you again?"

I told her my name, and reassured her that we weren't selling anything. She reluctantly agreed to let us in. We asked to see photographs and persuaded Evelyn to bring out an album. It lay flat on the coffee table in front of us.

"What do you want?" Evelyn kept asking, looking at Susan.

After Susan and I left, I returned to Evelyn's house with a bowl of blackberries. We sat, not talking.

•

We share a view. The back of our house meets the front of her house. We share a street, and the bikes that ride it, and a plump gray cat named Aubergine who tidies herself in the crook of the road. We share a taste for blackberries and chocolate chip cookies. We throw water at things, and hope that they'll grow.

Fear

Back then I lived alone on the North side of town, in a cabin on acreage overlooking a cliff. Built from cinderblocks, with a mossy thatched roof, the cabin was heated with a single small stove. The kitchen sink and shower emptied graywater into the field out back. The previous tenant had raised two llamas; in winter, they slept by the clawfoot tub.

It was the year my father learned he had cancer. I was flying out East on weekends, some weeks. At first I bribed friends to care for my dogs, but this began to feel awkward. So when I found a card in a coffee shop advertising pet sitting visits to the rural North side, it seemed like a gift. Rita and I met once in person. She was good with my dogs, soft-spoken, sincere. I trusted her, and she liked the cabin. She wasn't afraid, like some of my friends.

On one of my last visits to see my father, my flight home was delayed for hours. When I finally arrived back at the cabin, I had trouble negotiating the long, unlit drive. The only thing sparking the velvety dark was a plane overhead, glowing as it angled down over the trees.

I parked in tall grass by the front door and jingled my keys so the dogs would bark. Inside, relieved to be home and surrounded by scrambling dogs, I fumbled for the light on the opposite wall.

When the light snapped on, I stood silent, staring. I wanted to scream, but my mouth wouldn't move.

My bed was tucked into a corner facing the stove. Covering the bed was a zebra-striped quilt. On top of the quilt were a dozen small pillows: hot pink and bright blue; velvet, velour.

At the foot of the bed was a thick, soft rug that matched the zebra that had died on my bed.

Beside the bed was a wicker table holding a green glass vase full of fake flowers. Draped across the doorway was a pink-and-green boa.

The dogs. I knelt down and clung to their fur. Surely if someone was hiding in the back room the dogs would have alerted me by now? Cell phone in hand, I dialed 9-1.

Then logic set in. Criminals didn't add things to houses; they took stuff. Nothing was missing; it just looked as if a teenage girl had vomited the contents of her bedroom onto my bed.

On tiptoe, as if that would protect me, I edged under the boa and into the back room.

This time, furniture: two wicker chairs. More pillows, more zebras. A giant stuffed horse.

My kitchen table was covered with gauzy pink cloth, so it took me a minute to see the note.

Dear Carol,

Your sweet puppies were such good babies! I loved them up. So well-behaved!

You remind me of my daughter, Eileen. Same color hair and same color eyes. She would've liked this cabin, your funny face dogs. She liked nature, too, riding horses and such.

Fifteen years old. I looked a lot like her. Car accident, almost two years ago. Quilt, pillows, chairs: these were her things. I should keep them, enjoy them. Cheer the place up.

The dogs seemed fine; happy, in fact. In love with the rug, which was covered in dog fur, and the only thing I didn't take to Goodwill the morning after my night with Eileen.

The Secret Life of His Piano

Chopin begins at seven sharp. We wonder who he is, our pianist neighbor. Students trek in and out during the day. Their faltering scales catch in the leaves while their mothers read or nap in the car. At night our neighbor's lights illuminate black compost bins. Tchaikovsky and Mozart float over the street.

One evening, Elizabeth and I are driving home from work when we notice a red pickup parked in front of our house. A tall man with long pale hair strides through our yard. Something about the way he moves suggests to Elizabeth that she should pull over. We watch from a distance as the stranger approaches the driver's seat of the pickup truck. Maybe the engine's gone sour; maybe he'll kick a tire. Instead he wrenches open the door and grabs the driver by her curly hair.

Drags her. She resists, but he's rougher, pulls her onto asphalt. Kicks her. Raises his fist to hit her. Hits her. Elizabeth and I are frozen, afraid to intervene, when our neighbor runs into the street and stops in front of the man's raised fist.

He's thin, the pianist. We've never seen his face, just know the music he makes, and his students' mistakes. He stands firm, as if the street will save him, and yells at Red Truck to stop beating her up.

The Jumper

Home has a second story. I'm upstairs, working in my tiny attic office, when the front door creaks. Must be my partner, Elizabeth, who's taken our dogs to the park down the block.

To the landing, where I call Elizabeth's name. No sign of our boisterous dogs. The door's ajar; two people are talking on the stoop. Two people? We're notoriously anti-social; guests require careful plans. I'm confused, and start to walk downstairs when a short, sturdy man steps into the foyer.

He doesn't see me. He's in a leather jacket. I have no idea who this man is. Next, a much younger woman steps into the house behind him. She's in a mini-skirt and heels, a low-cut top.

I duck behind the banister at the top of the landing. It's a sunny afternoon. They've used a key. The man hesitates, doubles back for the door. The woman catches his arm, says something in Russian.

They stand speaking back and forth. He seems freaked out; she seems cajoling. Finally she walks toward the bedroom. As they enter the hallway, my view disappears.

Our house is as tall as most. I'll survive the jump if I leap, I know. Breaking a leg seems a small price to pay for surviving a home invasion by the Russian mob.

I slide the window back and remove the screen. I'm tangled in fear, logic, and flight. No one's around, so I can't call for help. If the criminals hear me, that's it; I'm toast.

What I can't figure out is what they'd want to steal. Most of our stuff is from thrift stores. Elizabeth collects books and mannequin parts; I collect damaged animals and other people's family photos.

I'm halfway out the window, one foot on the roof, when I catch a word of English: "tile."

I duck back inside. Walk down the stairs.

"Hi," I say, extending my hand to the tile makers who are scheduled to re-tile our damaged shower next week. "Sorry. I didn't hear you come in."

The woman smiles. "I'm Lexy," she says, "and this is my father, Ivan. The plumber left us a key in the mailbox. We tried to call, but you didn't answer. We're a few days early. I hope that's okay. We didn't want to interrupt your sewing."

"My sewing?"

Lexy points to a mannequin propped up naked in a corner. There's a mannequin head over the fireplace and an arm over the couch.

"The head scared my father. He thought you were something . . . not so good. But I explained that you must be a seamstress."

Everyone waits for my lie, for my "yes."

God Loves a Parade

The border guard was polite and businesslike. "What will you be doing in Canada?"

Elizabeth and I had rehearsed at home. No jokes about politics, no mention of same-sex marriage. Just the facts: we were meeting Elizabeth's father and stepmother in Vancouver for lunch.

Canada waved us in, more enthusiastic about our visit than Elizabeth's father. Actually, we hadn't heard from him directly at all. Dawna, Elizabeth's stepmother, had sent the greeting card that orchestrated the visit, signing it "Dan & Dawna" in flowery script. They were stopping in Vancouver, BC on the final leg of a church-sponsored Alaskan cruise. Elizabeth and I live an hour away from Vancouver, across the US border. A visit seemed both unwelcome and unavoidable.

Elizabeth's father was new to the Fundamentalist Christian lifestyle of cruises, vacations in exotic locales, and women named Dawna who bought his-and-hers cards. He'd been an average guy when he'd helped bring Elizabeth to life, providing sperm with little guilt. After an early and bitter divorce he became tons of fun, sampling drugs, alcohol, womanizing, and gambling. This phase lasted until Elizabeth was fifteen, and came out to him. Then God pointed an accusatory finger.

"He was lonely," Elizabeth explained, when I asked how he'd metamorphosed from Dad to The Gambler to God's Messenger. "He got a teaching job in a small town in California headed up by Fundies. They run atheists out of town after dark. At first he just went along with it so he wouldn't stand out, but when he started dating Dawna, she got him hooked."

In some small way I understood. As a kid my father moved our family all across the country. I learned to transform myself, to fit in with whatever hierarchy dominated each school. Never a question of being popular, it was purely a question of survival: how not to get beaten up in the bathroom or forced to drink sour milk in the cafeteria.

Maybe Elizabeth's father became a Fundie so he wouldn't get pummeled by the football coach.

"I think he just wanted to have someone to talk to. God was low on his list, but sometimes you draw low."

We talked it over as we drove through the farmland separating rural Washington from its cosmopolitan Canadian cousin.

"Maybe he'll love me today," Elizabeth said. "Maybe it's all going to be different this time."

"We are married here. Maybe they'll finally grasp that."

The exit to the parking garage landed us in the stuffy lobby of the wrong hotel. We poured ourselves wrong hotel coffee in the wrong hotel lobby before sashaying through the revolving door. Down the street, up two blocks, and there it was: hotel du jour. We shoved ourselves through another revolving door and contemplated revolving right back out. Trapped beside us were two fags in shorts and sleek black sunglasses. They smiled at our mutual smoosh.

Then there we were, in the lobby of the hotel. Elizabeth glanced around. I looked for halos, past a guy hovering in that creepy hotel lobby way.

"Elizabeth?"

Hovering man approached us. He seemed guarded, literally: nine or ten people followed him, surrounding him. The pack was dressed in matching shirts: a sturdy poly-cotton blend, sparkling white with a gold cross and Church of Something Really Big embroidered in red.

"Dad?"

Father and daughter just stared. The hug that didn't happen kept not happening.

"Dad? Carol and I are excited about meeting you and Dawna for breakfast."

"We've already eaten breakfast, but there's a McDonald's around the corner."

"No McDonald's," I whispered to Elizabeth. "I love you, but this I cannot do."

"Never mind, Dad. We don't need to eat."

The group smiled a collective smile. "Well, then," someone said.

Elizabeth and I started down the street. The pack followed, arranging itself around Dan and Dawna, who'd arranged themselves neither beside us nor behind us, but in between. After a block I realized that this was on purpose, lest we throw ourselves in a heap on the sidewalk and fuck on the street.

"Thimbles!" Dawna chirped as we passed a gift shop. Did we know she had a thimble collection? We did not. While she was rummaging through the store, Elizabeth bummed a cigarette off a passer-by. In the midst of this we started hearing things. Both of us, as if sharing a dream.

"Is that techno?"

The music got louder.

We wished ourselves back home, at our favorite club in Seattle, surrounded by sweaty dykes and perfumed drag queens. We could practically smell beer and what-all-else. We could practically see lithe men in hot pants and suddenly there they were, on top of a float.

"What's today's date?" I asked Elizabeth.

She smiled. "God loves us."

Dawna and Dan emerged from the shop with a bag of thimbles. Their Fundie friends were pointing and smiling, smiling and laughing at the merry-go-round of floats, pretty girls in dresses, handsome men in tuxes. Our happy, bright world.

It took a few minutes for the truth to sink in.

One by one their smiles slid off.

Vancouver, B.C.'s pride parade attracts thousands of people each year. This year that number was augmented by twelve homophobes and two lesbian newlyweds. Trapped in a swarm of gleeful onlookers, we had to wait for the parade to sashay past. The Fundies clustered around Dawna's thimbles, holding them up to the light, studiously ignoring the noise and the glitter of the parade, ignoring handfuls of candy and beads tossed as if from heaven.

As the last float straggled off, its homo cowgirls waving a lassoed goodbye, we said our own goodbye to Dan and Dawna and the whole live Fundie crew.

Driving back to the U.S. we got stuck at the border. At last our car reached the guard's glass window.

"Do you have anything to declare?"

"No," we both said.

My Father in Water

My girlfriend's father remembers a birthday, the unsigned cake of the daughter he's lost. He licks an envelope, thumbs a stamp. A gift comes wrapped in pink-and-gold paper. We watch the DVD he sends her: A man walks through the woods, holding a child. As it begins to rain he feels God's presence. He talks to the camera about God's plans for his son. The film is slick, MTV meets Leviticus, meant to bring a prodigal daughter back to the fold. To fold the envelope and fold her cards. His little syllepsis. It's meant to undress us, redress us in shame.

In another town my father drinks water. The water bleeds through a hole in his lungs. My father is drowning from the inside out. He has weeks to live, as I have weeks to know him.

The way I learn that my father has gone into the hospital is an email headed "New Symptom 12/13." As his lungs fill with fluid, he diagnoses himself. He sends the message to a few fellow scientists. Then he sends it as an email to me.

My girlfriend's father was born-again. Or is. Is born. Evangelical. I imagine him wading into the water wearing safety goggles and a brand new wife. He was an artist. Or is. He carves. His sculptures take up space outdoors. I know I'd like him—this artist, this teacher—if he didn't pretend that his daughter was dead.

❖

On-screen: snow. My father, breathing. A snow globe, shaken. His wintery lungs.

❖

My girlfriend says she's jealous of the father I have.

I tell her jealousy is a loaded gun, mouth dangerous as mine.

She says no mouth is as dangerous as mine.

❖

Thirteen days after we move into our new home, a two-bedroom bungalow in a two-horse town, wooden stakes appear on the lawn. Our neighbors have planted them, marking the line.

"Were you sunbathing naked on the neighbors' front lawn?"

"Would you like me to?"

"Stakes seem hostile."

"This is too familiar, our distracted neighbors."

"They will ice us out," she says of their chill.

I think of Indiana, where they ran us out, or tried: the Martinsville KKK arriving at a gay rights' meeting to blockade the doors. Walking home in twilight a car passed us and jumped the curb, aiming for our entwined arms. We spun off into a ditch and the car missed us. We rolled over and over, down the hill in the dark.

I think of Nebraska, where they burned us out, or tried: my girlfriend and I occupying the top floor of a rickety Victorian, peering out our bedroom window at the threats below.

We watched for the match.

We were always burning.

⁘

"Girlfriend" is not the same as "wife."

⁘

We do all the things our neighbors imagine. We fuck and fuck and fuck and fuck, sometimes forgetting to keep the windows closed. We forget to wear clothes when we take out the trash. The curves and angles of our bungalow symbolize a postwar/prewar dream of abundance. We decorate with photographs of strangers, odd bits of cloth, and mannequins Elizabeth stole in her previous life.

Her life of lying, juggling women. Fucking straight women behind their husbands' backs.

❖

The new wife presses the back of his shoulders, her hand between blades, imagining wings.
We say "love."
They say "Amen."

❖

"Carol Ann," says my girlfriend.
"Elizabeth Jane."
I would like, we both say (gun-shy, tongue-tied).
I would like very much for your hand in mine.

❖

My parents met as exchange students in Germany, where they fell in love in a foreign tongue. Always waiting on the verb, they began relying more and more on proper nouns, until their names filled each other's mouths like the secret machines of a fast-moving future.

Elizabeth's parents divorced young. In photographs she leans against the leather upholstery of a speeding car, dark circles underneath her eyes. Heartbroken, her father found God, who procured for him a cold widow to wed.

Elizabeth's mother was born again. In bed. After the divorce her sinuous legs slipped around her new boyfriend's neck like a noose. She was twenty-five; her boyfriend, eighteen. Elizabeth's mother did not have children. She hid her ghost children—my girlfriend, her brother—in the far back room of their rusty trailer.

She's reaching for something. I see her do it, I watch, and the whole thing happens again.

Elizabeth imagined a devoted mother. A mother who wouldn't let her new boyfriend touch her, crabapple hands at the hem of her skirt.

Back then we were strangers daydreaming about girlfriends like the ones we've become, girls with skirts and words always lifting, ballooning into a future filled with hothouse flowers. We were strangers, but grew up so close I could nearly touch her across the marshy fields of our South Carolina summers. Our families held damp, maudlin reunions in adjacent South Carolina counties. We're distantly related, Brabham to Bamberg to Barnwell. Cousins, fourth we think, but it isn't our cousinness that prevents our marriage.

Elizabeth, sewing a skirt to be ripped. And you of the sinuous legs—her mother. Not speaking to your lesbian daughter. Turning away from the streams of her wrists, from the disease you gave her, the dis-ease of sex.

❖

We are a couple who fuck.

Our neighbors build fences around the stakes. We burn candles and toast. We set a mannequin head in the window to watch their shenanigans.

❖

Growing up in South Carolina, my father climbed trees with his best friend and cousin, Bobby. They wore ghost costumes they'd found in Bobby's attic, costumes that Bobby's mother snatched away as soon as she saw them.

"Not for outside," she told the boys.

The ghost costumes were KKK robes. The boys folded the robes, put them back in the trunk.

❖

My father calls me "Cal" and "Bear." He's gentle, soft spoken. In hospital the doctors know him as a doctor, too. They whisper outside his room: Dr. Guess invented this and that vaccine, these statistical models for cancer research. What they don't say: they are using his research, not to cure him, but to buy him time.

I write a letter to Elizabeth's father. I tell him she's proud of him, proud of his art. I describe the garden we've started out back, and the cleverness of our blind dog, who has discovered, dog-like, digging. I describe him:

Rainer tilts his head to determine the angle of sun or shade. Then he sniffs around the plot, muzzling earth, uprooting black-berry brambles and bits of wood. When he's dug himself silly he rolls on his back in a flurry of dirt.

We don't hear back. Still I catch her with her hand in the mailbox, fumbling as the lid nips like teeth.

We are heat to seek.

We are cousins and strangers.

Our born-again President wants us to disappear.

❖

While my father is learning how to breathe underwater I begin taking yoga classes in a heated room. One hundred degrees, I think, of solitude. I send each breath over the miles to him.

One day I become sick, the heat dusting my lungs with panic, my careful balance dissolving in waves. I leave the room and find myself crying. Tears are just water, I think to myself.

I am learning about heat and how to stand up straight, taking on the language and traditions of a country I know nothing about, appropriating an ancient practice in order to stay in (American) shape.

My father breathes in and out, shaking with the newness of consciousness.

❖

If Elizabeth leaves me, I'll roll far away. I have it all planned—the mileage, the alias. I'll change my blue eyes, my inquiring name.

When I tell her this, she sees my father in me—his creativity in service to optimism but haunted by melancholia. I grew up knowing my father had chosen my mother in part because she isn't, ever, melancholy. She's a happy woman, stable and steady. Social and pretty. He chose her to handle him, to manage his depression. I grew up knowing that I'd have to manage mine alone, because I was female, because that's what women do. They take care of others. And I try—I do—but sometimes—

❖

my crooked tooth
my crooked way with women and words

❖

My parents chose the name Carol because it was the blandest name possible, offensive to no one.

But they considered another option. A name that swelled, cymbals and trumpets: Alexandria.

City of art, libraries, and pleasure.

City of my conception.

My secret name.

❖

Elizabeth dreams. Wakes up still dreaming. Speaks to me while I'm still asleep. "Your father," she says, "was explaining something. Everyone listened, but no one understood."

While we are trying to wake up, to listen, the phone rings.

My mother.

"Your father," she starts.

I hang up the phone.

The day of my father's death December breaks into snow, and January breaks through the last of December. My father dies on New Year's day, a few days after his birthday, a few days before mine.

Strange overlap—this is snow and this is a daughter and this is a father dying too soon.

⁘

Flying South the plane lurches, rump up, nose down. As it veers among clouds for once I feel, not fear but release. If I die now, I think, I can likely catch up.

I've seen several ghosts in my life, been haunted twice, and not found the experience especially pleasant. My father, too, once experienced a haunting. It surprised me to hear him tell it, traces of a Southern accent: a dream of water, swimming, and in the morning, news that his beloved swim coach, Bobby's father, had died at midnight in his sleep.

Elizabeth and I step off the plane, into Carolina heat. For the first time my father isn't there to meet me. Someday it will feel as if it has always been this way: My mother alone, grown smaller, hunched in a plastic chair in the machine-dream of an airport terminal.

My beautiful mother.

I remember my father slipping his arm around her shoulders: "The most beautiful woman," he'd say, "in the world."

We go out to dinner, three and not four of us.

"What should I call you?" my mother asks us, twisting a napkin into origami.

We are best friends and lovers and heat in the dark. What word should we form in another one's mouth?

"I hate the word partner," Elizabeth and I say in unison. A word tainted by commerce, clinical, cold. De-sexing us as the world would like it.

But who is this "we," this union of women?
"Why not wife?"
"Why not cousin?"

❖

We are Deep South. We are bound to heat. We are sweat, and tobacco, and our families owned slaves.

❖

"I am now of the age," Elizabeth announces, "when people die." She begins haunting the cemetery, looking for plots with two women, unrelated, buried side-by-side.

❖

On the sour break of hill behind my house, on my midmorning jog, on an ordinary day, in terrible sweatpants and mismatched socks, I'm suddenly stopped by four boys and a gun. I don't even pause; I turn, stupidly, to cruise control and keep running, the wings of my shoulder blades pursed, expecting a shot.
My father saves me.
I'm sure of it.
I feel him, absolutely present, and run all the way home, home alive to my girl.

❖

My father pointing
look at that
starling
as if as if
heaven
I'm here I said
turning

My father returns again and again. He is beside me in the car while I sing, off-key, to the sort of country music (the real stuff) he favored. He is beside me. I feel it so fiercely that I rest my right hand on the passenger's seat.

❖

Driving home one evening I notice a tiny motorcycle affixed to the side of a narrow bridge. Come Easter, there's a stuffed rabbit and a plastic egg. Come Christmas a cross, cut from black Styrofoam, fixed to tangled metal at the mouth of what really should be shoulder. For every season there's a memento, rough and handmade. One day I see her carrying something heartlike. Heartsick. It's February 14th. She hugs the metal guardrail as she walks to the center of the bridge. She sets the stained-glass circle around the cross like a halo.

I pull over just past the Death Bridge, wanting to touch her or cry together. I want this the way I always want something from women, the way as a girl I loved my best friend.

She stares at me coldly.

I drive on, not feeling my father at all.

❖

My father's mother died during labor, her blood sugar thick with sweet Southern cane. Sweet potatoes, brown sugar and cream. My father did not see his mother alive but was born through her death, shaken into inheritance. His father died a few years later, of prostate cancer. Harry Senior married his dead wife's sister. Harry Junior was raised by his aunt, now his mother. In truth he was lonely, half-raised by Bobby's father, half-raised by his family's impoverished gardener.

The gardener's name was Queenie. He had no last name. He was dark-skinned, and kind, and had a way with flowers.

My father's aunt, now his mother, was raised by a father who'd been burned out by Sherman.

My father, playing alone in an elaborate garden. His aunt, now his mother, wringing her hands.

As he lay dying I washed his feet. I uncurled the toes that lay cramped without feeling. I tended to him as he'd tended to children, neonates in isolation and two daughters at home.

He was logical, a scientist. He was not a man of superstition. So the words that coalesced on my lips surprised me. I knew—I know—he loved me. And I knew, in those moments, that I'd see him again.

What I told him, I told him silently. I let my thoughts blur into his. Your mother, I told him. Your mother is waiting.

It's time.

She knows you.

You'll know her strong hands.

⁘

Elizabeth means "Oath of God."

She should have been Jane, the usual name for the first-born girl in her family for generations.

But her mother's secret, her lie life, her shame!

Elizabeth was not the first-born girl but second to a dispossessed sister. Her ghost sister haunts her, holding onto her name.

⁘

Elizabeth calls her father on his fifty-ninth birthday. He talks about rain, his stepson, his wife. She waits, patiently. She breathes through the mouthpiece. She's waiting for "Carol," "roommate," or "friend."

He does not mention my name, my letter.

She is dead to him.

I am not yet born.

My father begins following me home, beside me in the

car for a time, then disappearing as I pull into the drive. His presence absorbs me. I want to unfold.

I wonder if what remains after death is love, abstracted into some form of ether or snow or animal sounds. If the blind dog's snores are an old man's snores, an old man who lived in Bamberg all his life, whose wife woke one day and made coffee and slipped on her puffy blue-and-violet house dress, stubborn slippers over calloused feet, before realizing he had stopped breathing sometime in the night. And maybe the first thing she thought of when she shook his shoulders was the first time they danced together, her heels and his uniform, and he was off to war soon, and might never return.

⁘

They choose Friday the 13th as their wedding day to prove to the world they are not superstitious. To cut ties with the Old World of Southern tradition and enter the Modern World of machines.

At the small, simple ceremony my mother is proud and more than a little scared, bewildered by the newness of the tight gold ring.

My father is already looking ahead, thinking of diseases he would like to cure, puzzle pieces in an endless string of numbers leading to the great equation.

He kisses my mother, the only woman he will ever love, his great beauty, his bride.

He longs for her.

He will cure diseases.

He sees cells dividing, the great pattern of things.

One more kiss, then.

"I know I'll see you again."

My father marries my mother on the same day he graduates from college with two degrees, the same day he enters the Navy.

He is twenty-three.

He will live forever.

Acknowledgements

These essays first appeared as follows: 'Aperture,' *Femme's Dictionary*, Calyx Books, 2004; and *Jabberwock Review*, Winter 2005; 'Evelyn,' *Brevity*, Fall 2010, Issue 34; 'Girl of Yes, and An End to Highways,' *Front Porch Journal*, Issue 4, October 2007; 'My Father in Water,' *Blue Mesa Review*, Issue 19, Spring 2007; 'Of Quarterbacks and Quarantine,' *Queer Girls In Class*, Peter Lang Publishing, 2011; 'On Carnival Lights, Compression, and Mice,' *The Rose Metal Press Field Guide to Writing Flash Nonfiction*, Rose Metal Press, forthcoming; 'Reading And Teaching *The Terrible Girls*,' *Fifty Gay and Lesbian Books Everybody Must Read*, Alyson Books, 2009; 'Red,' *Fourth Genre*, Vol. 2, No. 2, Fall 2000; *Gaslight*, Odd Girls Press, 2001; *Tell It Slant*, 2004; and *Five Years of Fourth Genre*, Michigan State University Press, 2006; 'Suspect: On Heather Lewis's *The Second Suspect*,' *American Book Review*, Vol. 31, No. 2, Jan/Feb 2010; 'Thoughts on Prose Blocks as Dance and Resistance,' *The Rose Metal Press Field Guide to Prose Poetry*, Rose Metal Press, 2010.

Thanks to Susanne Antonetta, Kimberly Balsam, Mykie Curtis, Scott Herring, Daniela Olszewska, Kerry Maddox Regan, Debra Salazar, and Julie Marie Wade.

Special thanks to my mother, Geraldine Guess, and my sister, Alison Guess Fitton.

Special thanks to Elizabeth J. Colen for everything.